DIZZY DOCTOR RIDDLES

Joanne E. Bernstein and Paul Cohen

Pictures by Carl Whiting

ALBERT WHITMAN & COMPANY, Niles, Illinois

Also by Joanne E. Bernstein and Paul Cohen

Creepy Crawly Critter Riddles

Grand-Slam Riddles

Happy Holiday Riddles to You!

More Unidentified Flying Riddles

Riddles to Take on Vacation

Sporty Riddles

Touchdown Riddles

Unidentified Flying Riddles

What Was the Wicked Witch's Real Name?
and Other Character Riddles

Text © 1989 by Joanne E. Bernstein and Paul Cohen
Illustrations © 1989 by Carl Whiting
Published in 1989 by Albert Whitman & Company,
5747 West Howard Street, Niles, Illinois 60648
Published simultaneously in Canada
by General Publishing, Limited, Toronto
10 9 8 7 6 5 4 3 2 1

Library of Congress Cataloging-in-Publication Data

Bernstein, Joanne E.
  Dizzy doctor riddles/Joanne E. Bernstein and Paul Cohen;
illustrated by Carl Whiting.
      p.   cm.
  Summary: A collection of more than 100 riddles about medical care
and diseases both real and imagined, including "What do you call it
when you break out in tiny wristwatches? Small clocks."
  ISBN 0-8075-1648-1
  1. Riddles, Juvenile.   2. Health occupations—Juvenile humor.
3. Hospitals—Juvenile humor.   4. Diseases—Juvenile humor.
[1. Medical care—Wit and humor.   2. Diseases—Wit and humor.
3. Riddles.]   I. Cohen, Paul, 1945-   .   II. Whiting, Carl, ill.
III. title.
PN6371.5.B39418   1989   89-35392
818'.5402—dc20   CIP
                                                      AC

Merry Maladies

What do you call a fear of Santa?
Claustrophobia.

How do you know you have the upside-down disease?
Your nose runs and your feet smell.

What do you call a rash on your leg joints?
Kneesles.

What do you call it when you break out in tiny wristwatches?
Small clocks.

What disease do you get from playing too much basketball?
The hooping cough.

What happened to the man who drank varnish?
It polished him off.

What happened to the patient who swallowed a spoon?
He could hardly stir.

Why didn't the girl go to the doctor when she swallowed a clock?
She didn't want to alarm anybody.

What happened to the woman who climbed up the chimney?
She came down with a flue.

Sick Jokes

How would you survive if you cut off your left side?
You'd be all right.

Why do people come to like their warts?
They have a way of growing on you.

Do pneumonia patients make quick recoveries?
No, it takes a lung, lung time.

When do broken bones become useful?
When they start to knit.

What's the best way through a poison ivy patch?
Itch hike.

If an apple a day keeps the doctor away, what does an onion do?
It keeps EVERYONE away.

Why do some people get all the breaks?
They're clumsy.

What can you give away and still keep?
A cold.

How do you avoid that rundown feeling?
Look both ways before crossing the street.

Who takes pills that are half aspirin, half glue?
People with splitting headaches.

Where should you stay if you think you're dying?
In the living room.

BOB: I keep seeing spots before my eyes.
MARK: Have you seen a doctor?
BOB: No, just spots.

What's Up, Doc?

Why was the patient laughing after the operation?
The doctor had him in stitches.

How do doctors make money on the side?
By taking out appendixes.

How do doctors deal with amnesia patients?
They make them pay in advance.

Why did the doctor move the patient away from the window?
So he'd feel no pane.

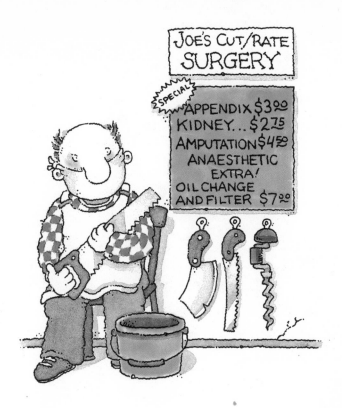

Why couldn't the surgeon make much money?
He ran a cut-rate operation.

Why are doctors often dizzy?
From doing rounds and rounds.

When can you get hurt following a doctor's prescription?
When it flies out the window.

Why don't doctors predict who'll get chicken pox?
They don't like to make rash promises.

What do you do when the doctor tells you to undress?
Just grin and bare it.

How does a doctor take apart her Christmas tree?
She performs a tinselectomy.

How did the urologist reach the top?
He climbed the bladder of success.

Whom should you call if there's a mouse in your clock?
The hickory-dickory doc.

What equipment do doctors take climbing?
Oxygen tents.

How do obstetricians like their mail sent?
Special delivery.

Which doctor was a real knockout?
The anaesthesiologist.

What state is a doctor?
MD (Maryland).

Filling No Pain

How should a dentist examine a crocodile's teeth?
Very carefully.

What did the dentist like best about the army?
All the drilling.

What do you say to a sick dentist?
"Hope you're filling better."

What is the dentist's favorite musical?
"Annie Get Your Gum."

What should you do when your tooth falls out?
Quick! Get the toothpaste!

What did the dentist want from the lawyer?
The tooth, the whole tooth, and nothing but the tooth.

What does the dentist say when you enter the office?
"Gum on in."

Jokes to Quack You Up

Where do mallards go after an accident?
To the ducktor.

Why don't they like that ducktor?
He's a quack with a big bill.

How did the rodent doctor save lives?
With mouse-to-mouse resuscitation.

Did he ever visit his patients at home?
Yes, he made mouse calls.

Why did the cat join the Red Cross?
To be a first-aid kit.

Where do you send a sick pony?
To the horsepital.

What do you do for a sick canary?
Have it tweeted.

What's gray, visits you when you're sick, and breaks a chair?
A get-wellephant.

Why do elephants have tusks that aren't straight?
Their parents can't afford braces.

What was the animal doctor after he treated the whales?
Soaking vet.

What disease does a dog get in its joints?
Arf-ritis.

Why did the hen go to the doctor?
For her annual chick-up.

Why did the rabbit go to the doctor?
He was feeling jumpy.

What do you give bald rabbits?
Hare tonic.

Hospital Horrors

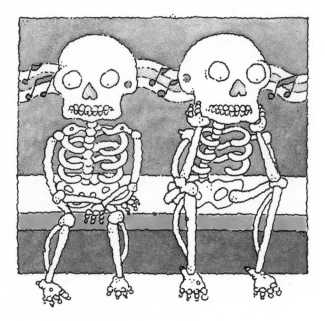

Why don't skeletons like hospital parties?
They have no body to dance with.

How does the doll surgeon operate?
It operates on batteries.

What does a vampire take when he has a cold?
Coffin drops.

What do robots take for coughs?
Robotussin.

Which doctor treats witches?
Witch doctor treats witches.

What kind of ship does Dr. Dracula prefer?
A blood vessel.

A-ward Winning Riddles

What's harder than making a child go to the hospital?
Making the hospital go to the child.

How did one sick kid get to the hospital?
He flu.

What *are* hospitals?
Places where run-down people wind up.

What plant grows in hospital rooms?
I.V.

Why did the garbage collector go to the hospital, Madam?
For a can, Sir.

What kind of dog do you find in a hospital?
A doc-shund.

Where does baby corn come from?
It's brought by the stalk.

What do you call bunk beds in the maternity ward?
Upper birth and lower birth.

Why did the pregnant movie star have an ultrasound test?
She wanted to see scenes from the coming attraction.

What did the hungry twins say in the womb?
Fetus, fetus (feed us, feed us).

Job Jabs

What do you say to a sick shepherd?
Get wool soon.

What do you say to a sick sailor?
Hope you're back on your fleet in no time.

What do you say to a sick oilman?
Get well soon.

What do you say to a sick dairy farmer?
Feel butter.

Why did the teacher go to the eye doctor?
He couldn't control his pupils.

What do you say to a sick lawyer?
Get will soon.

What happened to that sick lawyer?
He took attorney for the worse.

How do you stop a lawyer from bleeding?
With attorney-kit.

Why are astronauts always examined after they land?
In case they come down with something.

Why don't grape growers go to the doctor?
They always feel vine.

What does everyone say to the doctor?
A-a-a-h.

More Sick Jokes

PATIENT: Doctor, I think I'm a pretzel.
DOCTOR: Come to see me. I can straighten you out.

PATIENT: I have this terrible problem. I steal postage stamps.
DOCTOR: Don't worry—I'll help you lick it.

PATIENT: Doctor, will you treat me?
DOCTOR: No, you'll have to pay like everyone else.

PATIENT: Doctor, I have potatoes in my ears.
DOCTOR: How did that happen?
PATIENT: I don't know. I planted carrots.

DOCTOR: Your cough sounds much better today.
PATIENT: It should be. I practiced all night.

PATIENT: I keep thinking I'm a deck of cards.
DOCTOR: Sit down. I'll deal with you later.

PATIENT: Doctor, am I going to die?
DOCTOR: That's the *last* thing you'll do!

What did they call Jesse James when he had the flu?
A sick-shooter.

What do you call a successful injection?
A jab well done.

Why didn't the girl have her eyes checked?
She liked them plain blue.

How will they feed sick astronauts on our neighboring planet?
Intra-Venus-ly.

What did the sick banana tell its mommy?
I don't peel good.

What do blood testers see at dusk?
Red cells in the sunset.

What kind of injection hurts the most?
Pain-icillin.

What did the bus driver say to the nurse with the needle?
Step to the rear, please.

When is a nurse like a robber?
When she takes your temperature.

What nut is like a sneeze?
Cashew!

Mother: How do you want to take your cough
syrup?
Child: With a fork.

What's the difference between a hill and a pill?
One is hard to get up and the other is hard to get down.

In what country were bacteria discovered?
Germ-any.

What's the most dangerous part of a needle?
The end!